Discovering Ichthyosaurus

Written by Rena Korb
Illustrated by Ted Dawson

Content Consultant:
Kenneth Carpenter
Curator of Lower Vertebrate Paleontology & Chief Preparator
Denver Museum of Nature and Science

visit us at www.abdopublishing.com

Published by Magic Wagon, a division of the ABDO Publishing Group, 8000 West 78th Street, Edina, Minnesota 55439.
Copyright © 2008 by Abdo Consulting Group, Inc. International copyrights reserved in all countries. All rights reserved.
No part of this book may be reproduced in any form without written permission from the publisher.

Looking Glass Library™ is a trademark and logo of Magic Wagon.

Printed in the United States.

Text by Rena Korb
Illustrations by Ted Dawson
Edited by Jill Sherman
Interior layout and design by Emily Love
Cover design by Emily Love

Library of Congress Cataloging-in-Publication Data
Korb, Rena B.
  Discovering Ichthyosaurus / Rena Korb ; illustrated by Ted Dawson ; content consultant, Kenneth Carpenter.
      p. cm. — (Dinosaur digs)
   ISBN 978-1-60270-107-6
  1. Ichthyosaurus—Juvenile literature. I. Dawson, Ted, 1966- ill. II. Title.
QE862.I2K67 2008
567.9'37—dc22
                                2007034056

In 1699, the first drawings of Ichthyosaur (ik-thee-uh-sor) bones appeared in a book in England. Scientists did not know what animal the bones came from but thought it might be a fish. At the time, no one believed that sea reptiles as large as Ichthyosaur had ever lived.

In 1811, Mary Anning and her brother were collecting fossils on the beach in Lyme Regis along the southern coast of England. Joseph saw a strange shape in the rock. It turned out to be the skull of an ancient creature. Later, Mary, who was only 12 or 13 years old, dug out the creature's body. Mary sold the fossil, which was displayed at a museum.

No one knew what this creature was. Some people thought it was an ancient crocodile, bird, or fish. It took several years for scientists to realize this creature was an ancient sea reptile. In 1818, Charles Koeing named it *Ichthyosaurus*, which means "fish lizard."

Hong peered out the window of the inn. The rain had finally stopped! He had been cooped up inside for days, ever since he and his parents had arrived in England.

Hong grabbed his backpack. It held small tools, a notebook, a camera, and other items. Hong was not an ordinary kid—he was a dinosaur hunter.

Hong learned about dinosaurs from his father, who was a paleontologist. Hong had attended digs around the world and helped uncover fossils such as dinosaur bones. He had even discovered some fossils himself.

Now, Hong and his parents set out to explore the beach. They followed a path that led down a steep cliff. Hong's father explained that the coast of England was an important fossil graveyard.

The southern coast of England is called the Jurassic Coast. About 200 million years ago, a large sea covered the land. The bones of many creatures were left behind in the rocks and cliffs.

Hong's father also told him about a girl only a few years older than Hong. The girl became a famous fossil collector. "Her name was Mary Anning," he said. "Her family was poor, so she looked for fossils to sell. The tongue twister, 'She sells seashells by the seashore' is about her fossil hunting. She found the first complete specimen of a huge sea reptile called *Ichthyosaurus.*"

"It can't be as cool as dinosaurs," Hong muttered.

"Ichthyosaur prowled the seas while dinosaurs prowled the land," Hong's father said. "In fact, Ichthyosaur probably developed from a reptile that once lived on the land. Their arms and legs became flippers. It was even given a name before the first dinosaur. Do you remember that dinosaur's name?"

"*Megalosaurus,* named in 1824," said Hong, smiling proudly.

Ichthyosaurus was probably a fast swimmer. To drive itself forward, it moved its tail and its body from side to side. It used its front flippers to keep from rolling over.

On the beach, Hong and his parents followed a rocky shelf that ran along the bottom of the cliff. Hong soon wandered ahead.

While studying the sand and rocks, Hong noticed something unusual. Most people would have just seen a dirty-looking object, but Hong knew that ancient bones were brown, not white. He picked up his find—a thin, pointy tooth!

The mouth of the *Ichthyosaurus* was filled with many teeth. It used its sharp teeth to catch and bite through small fish, shrimp, squid, and other sea creatures.

Hong looked around, but he did not see any more teeth. Then he studied the nearby cliff to see if the tooth came from a buried fossil.

Hong saw a telltale line. "Dad, come quick! I think there's a fossil buried in the cliff!"

Like other reptiles, *Ichthyosaurus* had lungs. It rose out of the water to breathe air. Its nostrils were located far back on the snout, near the eyes.

Hong showed his father the tooth before wrapping it in a handkerchief and storing it in his backpack. Then, he pointed out the cliff face. Hong's father agreed. It was time to dig! They would need a hammer to chip into the hard rock.

"Good thing I have my kit," Hong said, opening his backpack.

"Don't forget your goggles and gloves," his mother reminded him.

Carefully, Hong used his hammer and chisel to tap at the rock. He worked a few inches around the cracks in the cliff face.

Soon, Hong found something. "It's a jawbone!" he cried. "I can see the teeth."

Hong stopped to take a picture. Like all paleontologists, when he came across an exciting find—especially an unexpected one—he documented it with pictures.

Hong continued to hammer. Small, sharp pieces of rock flew off the cliff face with each blow. Hong's goggles protected him. After awhile, Hong uncovered the rest of the jaw.

As Hong worked, his parents helped. His mother took pictures and his father wrote down what they saw in Hong's notebook. The notebook was filled with facts about the fossils Hong dug up.

A few more careful taps and Hong saw a bone curving around to form a large circle.

"This is where the animal's eye was," Hong's father said. "You know what I think you've found?"

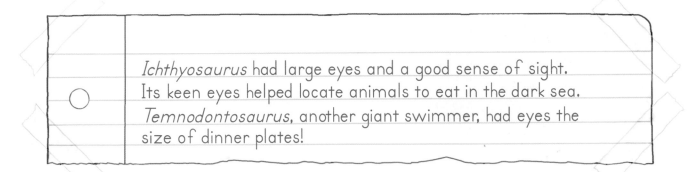

Ichthyosaurus had large eyes and a good sense of sight.
Its keen eyes helped locate animals to eat in the dark sea.
Temnodontosaurus, another giant swimmer, had eyes the size of dinner plates!

Hong looked hard at the skull. It had a pointy beak, a jaw filled with sharp teeth, and huge eyes. The skull did not look like any dinosaur he had ever seen. Besides, dinosaurs only lived on land. Maybe this strange fossil belonged to a bird or a fish.

Then he had an idea. "Is this *Ichthyosaurus?*" he asked. "Did we find the same sea reptile that Mary Anning found?"

Instead of laying eggs like most reptiles, *Ichthyosaurus* gave birth to live young. Scientists learned this when they found a fossil with the skeleton of a small *Ichthyosaurus* inside it.

When his father nodded, Hong grinned. "I take it back. *Ichthyosaurus* are definitely as cool as any dinosaur! I can't wait to see what the rest of it looks like!"

"Unfortunately, you're going to have to," Hong's father said, pulling out his cell phone. "I'm calling for help. This is a rare find, and we have to remove it before the tide comes in. Now that the skeleton is exposed, the waves could wash the fossil away."

In a short time, Hong saw a group of men and women making their way quickly down to the beach. Soon, they were hard at work.

Hong and his parents watched the race between the scientists and the tide. As the ocean water moved higher up the shore, the team uncovered the rest of the fossil. Then they spread thin, liquid glue over it. The glue would hold all the small bone fragments in place so they would not get lost.

Ichthyosaur	Dolphin
<ul><li>Reptile</li><li>Swam through the ocean</li><li>Long, beaklike mouth filled with teeth</li><li>Tail swept from side-to-side</li></ul>	<ul><li>Mammal</li><li>Swam through the ocean</li><li>Long, beaklike mouth filled with teeth</li><li>Tail moves up and down</li></ul>

While the scientists waited for the glue to dry, Hong had a chance to see his find. Except for its long snout, *Ichthyosaurus* looked like a dolphin. *Ichthyosaurus* and dolphins both have bodies that glide easily through the water. They also have long, beaklike mouths filled with teeth.

Ichthyosaurus had four flippers. The pair in front were longer than the pair in back. From its pointy snout to its skinny tail, it stretched about seven feet (2 m) long!

Once the glue was dry, the scientists took out large hammers and chisels. They chipped out the block that contained the fossil and removed it from the cliff face. Then, they wrapped it in burlap and plaster. Their work was done—and they had beaten the tide!

The scientists thanked each other and started to move down the beach. Some of them carried the huge piece of rock to the truck. They would take it to their fossil laboratory to study it more closely.

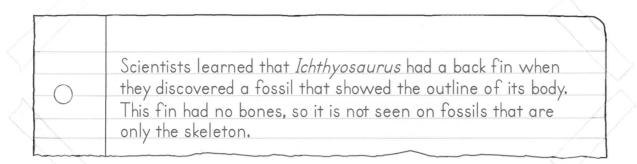

Scientists learned that *Ichthyosaurus* had a back fin when they discovered a fossil that showed the outline of its body. This fin had no bones, so it is not seen on fossils that are only the skeleton.

Suddenly, Hong thought of something. "Wait!" he called, running after them with his backpack in hand. He reached into it for the handkerchief that held the tooth—the tiny clue to the big fossil find. "Here's one of its teeth," he said.

The team stopped for a second. Then, a woman stepped forward and patted his shoulder. "You keep it, Hong," she said. "You deserve a souvenir of your find!"

In 2001, scientists discovered the world's oldest vomit. More than 160 million years ago, an *Ichthyosaurus* vomited up the shells of some of the animals that it had eaten.

ACTIVITY: Tools for Digging

What does a paleontologist use these tools for?

3. notebook

2. goggles

1. hammer

6. glue

5. chisel

4. camera

GLOSSARY

chisel — a metal tool for cutting, shaping, or chipping away wood or stone.

dig — a place where scientists try to recover buried objects by digging.

document — to make a record of something by writing about it or taking a picture of it.

face — the steep outer side of a cliff.

fossil — the remains of an animal or a plant from a past age, such as a skeleton or a footprint, that has been preserved in the earth or a rock.

paleontologist — (pay-lee-ahn-TAH-luh-jist) a person who studies fossils and ancient animals and plants.

souvenir — an object kept as a reminder of something.

specimen — a typical example of a kind of living thing.

READING LIST

Arnold, Caroline. *Giant Sea Reptiles of the Dinosaur Age.* New York: Clarion Books, 2007.

Brown, Don. *Rare Treasure. Mary Anning and Her Remarkable Discoveries.* New York: Houghton Mifflin, 1999.

Eldredge, Niles. *The Fossil Factory: A Kid's Guide to Digging Up Dinosaurs, Exploring Evolution, and Finding Fossils.* Lanham, MD: Roberts Rinehart Publishers, 2002.

Lessem, Dino Don. *Monsters of the Sea.* New York: Grosset & Dunlap, 2002.

ON THE WEB

To learn more about *Ichthyosaurus*, visit ABDO Publishing Company on the World Wide Web at **www.abdopublishing.com**. Web sites about *Ichthyosaurus* are featured on our Book Links page. These links are routinely monitored and updated to provide the most current information available.